languageslips

languageslips

Christopher Konrad

BLACK COCKIE PRESS

languageslips
Published by Black Cockie Press
Copyright © Christopher Konrad 2025
The moral right of the author has been asserted
Cover design © Natalie Muller 2025
Cover Image © Christopher Konrad
Distributed by IngramSpark
Printed by IngramSpark
ISBN: 978-1-7643294-0-8

About The Author

Christopher is a Western Australian writer. He has co-authored several poetry books, including Sandfire (Sunline Press, 2012) and Breath of the Sea (2012) with other WA poets. He has poems and short stories published in many journals, anthologies and online including Westerly, Southerly, Regime, Page Seventeen, Wet Ink, Creatrix, Swamp, Axon, Island, Cordite, Tamba. Along with many other awards he received First Prize for the Tom Collins Poetry Award (2009 & 2018) and the Todhunter Literary Award (2012) for a short story. He is published in Best Australian Poems 2013. He completed his doctorate in creative writing (2012) at Edith Cowan University. His books of poetry include Argot, (Pomonal, 2016) and Blind Summits (with Ross Bolleter) (Sunline Press, 2020). His latest collection of short stories The Voyeur (Balboa) was published in 2021. He is currently completed a collection of essay-meditations on being a migrant child.

Contents

MOTH

Prima Materia	13
Morning of the Magician	14
Remember the Aspidistras	15
Under the Agave	16
The Sea	17
Blind fish	19
Egret	20
Gulls	21
Menagerie	22
Paper bag	24
Scorpions	25
Millipede: via negativa	26
Moth	27
New birds	28
Response to an alien cartography	29
Black Mariah	31
War	32
The machinery of being	33
Great waves of Hokusai San	34
Merry-go-round	35
Pave the Way	36
Rule of God	37

Psalm 105	38
In the steps of Chief Joseph of the Nez Perce	39
I, John Clare	41
Meet you at the Opus 109	43
Liminal	45
Anywhere	47
Another entirely different road	48
Self-revealed	49
Found (*ad honorem Ross Seaton*)	50
Calvary (*after the movie*)	52
Anaphora	53
Memory Incinerates	55
Gleaming wears out the gaze	56
Corrode away	57
Water under the bridge (*after Lucy Ellmann*)	58
Seemliness	59

languageslips

I	63
II	64
III	65
IV	66
V	67
VI	68
VII	69
VIII	70
IX	71
X	72
XI	73
XII	74
XIII	75
XIV	76
XV	77
XVI	78

XVII	79
XVIII	80
XIX	81
XX	82

WATERS OF THE HEART

When I was young	85
Hard marrow	87
Heart	88
forget me, honey	89
Nearing	90
Refurbish	91
Letters to Milena	92
Letters to Ophelia Queiroz	93
Flowers of the mouth (*after Baudelaire*)	96
Fallen guy	98
Failed Whore	100
Asuntos del corazón	101
Waters of the heart	102
Va Pensiero	103
The Principle of Limitation (*after Bolleter*)	105
Busted piano man	107
A day in Marfa (*after Marfa Girl*)	109
Meeting at Tipasa	111
Port Talbot (*ad honorem Michael Sheen*)	112
Art rain	115
Mornington	116
Gwen Harwood's Nightfall	118
Oyster Cove	119
Hobart Town	121
Phoenix	122
Wintering with Sei Shōnagon	123
Lists	125
Kundera	127

De l'amour	128
Accept	130
Little gargoyle (*for Esther*)	131
Child's heart	132
Marj and Harvey (*in memoriam*)	133
Meditation upon Hexagram 32 Heng	135
Crazy man	137
Sun, Sun	138
Delight	139
Acknowledgements	140
Awards	141

MOTH

Prima Materia

Be the acorn to the oak   travel the river that
once stepped in is never the same one again   raw like
the day, like the chthonic caaarrrrkkkk of the bird of darkness
the intransigence of the moon crossed over Scorpio

Be like Scipio   great conqueror of Carthage
great general giving offerings at the Temple of Jupiter

Above all, be that acorn, tiny but great   that prima materia
Above all, have some savoire faire ...

Live your days as if your life depended on it
like you have something to say about it all   run your
commentary on the who and how   a good place
to dine, a good wine to drink and place to think

about progeny and legacy
how we can all eat at the same table once again

Morning of the Magician

Two boiled eggs for breakfast, no more, no less
the toast perfect and rainclouds gathering fast
I run to shut the windows   Another morning, mindless
aimless full of unfulfilled possibilities

Sometimes I think I'm a magician, hidden behind
a silk curtain, manipulating the world: drinking coffee, smoking
running several gauntlets of the living and the dead

The wind picks up, clattering gum nuts, mini branches
snapped-off, old, dead twigs and assorted storm debris which
attacks the tin roof like some giant hawk or crow with
talons sharp as a garden fork

Light trickles away with deepening sky, a tide going out
and the shadowy dark occupies my brain
I conjure cemeteries, ancestors, lost loved ones
who now gather to protect me: the day wind-blasted
the house suddenly fragile and I within it, a snail within a shell
about to be crushed by some giant boot

Remember the Aspidistras

It is said somewhere, I cannot remember by whom anymore · maybe it was a dream · that any book with the words 'Remember the aspidistras' in it would become a best seller · I think it was a book written by George Orwell or someone famous · In any case, those words led me to recalling, with not some little sadness or bitterness, the story of Michael and Joan · I'm not sure, but I think it may have been because of what I was going through at the time that this little story had such a profound impact on me · or perhaps it was the unhappiness of the words that dripped through like rain in a wheat field ripe for harvest and you knew the farmer's life would be destroyed by such an event · The one scene in that little book which, of course, moved everyone so deeply, and which most of us who have ever gone through a marriage breakdown could not but have been overwhelmed by, was the description the author gave of a forest scene · In that image the canopy of the forest was so thick it would not let any sky in, the sky which became torn with grief and then, the forest taking pity on her, decided to leave one small opening where several trees had been felled by a local for firewood · and there, a beam of sunlight shot through into that small space like a torchlight in the thick of midnight · It was there that Michael decided to sit on one of the felled logs and promised not to move until his true love would come · Which she did · That same day Joan had decided to leave her husband one final time, tears running hot down her red cheeks and her feeling as though they would never end, and she, lost in the wreckage of her unhappiness, thinking unbearable things · perhaps even to end her own life looks up suddenly in that one place in the dark forest lit up and radiant, she sees Michael sitting in the clearing and could think only to say, 'Remember the Aspidistras?'

Under the Agave

… the cat lies in a repose worthy of the days of Queen of Sheba and how many of these felines worshipped in those dusty days of antiquity. Under the Autumn grapes winter's tendrils surreptitiously dangle, dying leaves a falling chiaroscuro all around: *le chat* in the sun's flickering shade sleeps and dreams what? Perhaps the Age of the great creatures, her ancestors, that roamed and ruled in the cradle of humanities incipience. Nightmares follow the demise of the magnificent beasts: Sabre tooths, lions, tigers, Jaguars, panthers, pets of the demigod sovereigns of Egypt, Rome. Today, this slinky, silky diminutive creature curls, not so much on the laurels of days gone, on greatness, but rests with the ease of long-earned knowledge that still pulses puny humans on the whims of her paws and purrs. Her diminished guttural grrrrrr rattling in her sleep like a wretched last rasp.

The Sea

The Maternal Sea: fuck that

                          Elspeth Montrose

Do not go with ease into that Sea
Scream, screech at it and its scriveners   tear
at that untimely thing   *The Maternal Sea*, she clenched
through her gritted teeth, *fuck that!* Dylan and his father   you and
your mother, do not cry but rail against the oncoming of it

Whoever declared this wet nurse Ocean, mother of us all?   Rather
be Canute who commands it: back to from whence ye come
grand impostor   Unmake me, I dare you, leviathan architect

Briny thing, watery grave, usurper from which we all have crawled

By what names know thee: Undina's Aria, the Deep, the Depths, Oceanic, the Vast, the Big Blue, the Hungry, the Salt, Tempestuous Mistress, Roaring Fury, Rhythm of the Tides, Stella Maris, how she yelps, howls, rigging's eternal whines, endless wailing, the Sirens call, Cradle of Life, whale road, Charybdis & Scylla, all womb

But how sweet those pinks and Barbie typewriter, ephemeral ribbons
apart from the *fuck that*   Be my mother impossible woman

sapphic, sweet, scathing, correct   The cheery dark, Lesbos dreams,
anchorage at a safe shore   Amazons of the Greeks and
the Dahomey of Africa

Let bygones begone and mothers too
need to get on with things

Blind fish

The water stirs   a blur of stars
in the depths of I don't know when

Blind fish feels the push of it
against its gills   its scale-skin
pushes forward with a flick of its ancient
tail as saline liquid rushes by   a kind of ecstasy

She halts, wavers

What do you see blind thing?   Cave walls
gold, blue, umber   all colours of the oceans
wrapped around, unseeing, yet knowing
in the way we know   eyes all shut

Strutting this dry stage where ghosts visit
in the night   I look for the door
the way out   beyond into clear day and
water stirs all around

Egret

In the night the fragile bird imagines her flex of wing
feather fanned to show love, the chatter of neck and
impeccability of mandible: avian mind firmly fixed
skyward in the dive, the flare   graceful landing

Egret mounts her deliberate vision in the obsidian night
knowing neither dark nor light
Need as method of being   swoop swirl sway

She imagines nature's imperative as morning rises
out of the mist over the lake   sharp reeds caress
wind and water stitch the tapestry of evening into dawn
as the majesty bird lifts out of her nest

Gulls

Gulls wheel around the mountain   Kunanyi

at its base glassed-in verandahs to hold back certain

and uncertain histories on this dark island   Clouds flighty

as the birds winged high dropping

scootering in over the city squawking, crying for more

or less

Still, the fish, mussels are fine for cracking open

with steel-beaks   Where is there another Jonathon Livingstone

amongst them? Restless, chatty birds   fishers of men

one-legged bandits, perennial sign of sea and salt   sifting air

Pour me a water   Do not let the city's laws adjust you

Cry for me when the weather is finished with us

Kunanyi - Mt Wellington, Tasmania

Menagerie

Bird

Bird points the way

morsing print-messages in the baked sand

like an arrow   I am made clear

on a murky horizon   fly fly

into the grains that usurp tomorrow

which brings down the sun in its correct time

Mouse

Gender me this, mouse, in your cage

your Gulag   genes played as keys on a piano

Boy-girl, do you know? Trans this youthful path

your skin morphs and suddenly you are

Who are my ovaries to say you are not and yet

gender me this grey, furry, little being

make me know because

the shore of my unknowing is stretched long

and rough: but you know, don't you, in your Siberia

Will you make it through the Winter on you own?

Train

Iron thrust   push it hard this horse-powered thing
over wooden sleepers, pins, and gravel   shake,
tremble   let the hot air bullet past windows and
trees, shrubs, hillocks, fleeting gauntlet to my self-assurance
what did I see? Lift the game metal-horse, sing along this
shiny steel road Geomancer, remake my world in streaky vision

Let the steel be my guide before I go off the rails

stations ahead mark my life: tread effortlessly
be my Batman, dark machine
be my Eurydice and I will come and find you
my cage, my menagerie   Hold me tight
do not let my fragile body loose upon its many themes or
perhaps be my only compass
my last and only Way

Paper bag

Little brown bag, flutterby: the breeze catches your lip. Little-she looks where to launch you, your home, the place to where little bag leads. Tables and chairs like hieroglyphs: the sun brings its kindness this day and the walk over has done me good.

Open the skies for this child: to whom make this address and now, give pause to realities of the fold: fold and flap little paper bag, Undo this weave and dissolve into before I sat here to eat this pie and watch you reveal your work. Tomorrow: little girl in the world above this one and towards which we all will float.

Scorpions

Under stones air thickens · silence congeals
dust in a sealed jar · the scorpion stirs, black as bone
all compression and waiting · its body written backwards

To face her · meet the night in day
shadow hard obsidian each joint a refusal
each claw, hunger held too long · her sting an afterthought
of language charmed · a hooked query
Deserts teach patience · a slow calculus of thirst

She must flatten · learn to vanish
does not hurry but carries within the rhythm of collapse
has seen rivers arid, villages emptied, walls crumble into sand
her steps are small and precise · her sting curved above
poised not in anger but in punctuation older than words

We call it venom, but perhaps it is only memory condensed
earth's bitterness distilled into a single drop
poisons we mistake for protection, truths we keep curved
inside us like questions we will never ask

Millipede: *via negativa*

Minute gargantuan · transcendent legs
I lift the leaf and you are there · the hoisted stone
uncovers you · I enter your fallen place and
am lifted too · your diminutive upholds the law ·
covert and beyond sight · your Ways intangible ·
your colour supreme · my ascended happiness abides

Hardened cloak tenebrous on your shoulders
dreich clouds dark with water above · Millipede
through the pall · my brightness juxtaposing heavy ·
Your being louder than the earth

Moth

Flow back, backwards, time · to the rear ye get, mighty river · undo the done, the yet to be · Fall into that mirror · into the dark, into the glimmer of toda · Keep me, winged beast, pinned to the board of cork · face down into that flattened bark · forever · the breath of dust on my abdomen and onlookers ooh and ahhh · keep me pinned · pitiful animal · The entomologist, the pin and me · moth of detritus · we, the new Koan of life · succumbed I stare into the abyss and the crowd closes in · Use this magnifying glass · see the hairs on the nape · see the non-reflective nano-structures on the surface of my eyes which prevent predators finding me · tis all a gloss in the end, is it not · the pretense of being · I say BE · like the moth · wing-pinned and incapable · an object of curiosity · the darkness rolling back · Daylight illumines all

New birds

Crows disappeared because of water stolen from wells dryer than an oven; rains retreat in dramatic inversion, void in these times lush with other Clouds, stretched across crenellated alien-blue: the skies are full of new birds, new rain washes over us – droning birds replace humming birds ... and so, parched earth in united chorus beseech these aviators of evolution, metal feathered come to feed my fields, bird shit and spit: grain modified for my advancement – trees splinter, stone cracks, roads end now.

Response to an alien cartography

Crows sound the alarm at all times of day but it's those held in conference with their murders that reveal the dark-sludge certainty of earths rattles: it is the corvine call to arms for those dumb to the kraaaaarck call of black beasties which point the way with black beaks shiny like armour and aimed like truth-knives at those nested in the halls of wanton power.

... thoughts seeded like grevillea birds swaddled in honey, drip drip dripping like tumblers emptying into flensed rib cage of a contagion reminiscent of plagues of past: skin slated with undecipherable codes like bird-prints and beak marks scoring an opera open to a deep deep night: stars dead yet shining like grinning million-year-old cadavers which have watched over us for longer than we have been simian-sapiens.

Hrab watch like black feathered towers over our personal declensions into a perfect maelstrom of purposelessness and idiot-repose. How is it we cannot curse those leathery saurian breeds escaped from chthonic ornithines of aeons past and which brought their dark speech into the world of us: their aaarrrckk-squawks seamed through the long millennia into the ears of monkeys which ape-mimed into sapiens lungs, larynx slipped onto lips and tongues finally scrawled into stone become speech and word and script.

I watched as willy wagtails crossed swords, zeroed in on dark leviathans, pluck coarse feathers to make nests, drop like leaves into the earth there to be planted in nightmares: expunge sweaty dreams from my sleepless nights: anointy ointy pointy birds, descendants of beast of pray and here to entertain my dreary mind and make fools of us all. Crows look back at diminutive ancient cousins and send out knives from bottomless eyes while little cousins fly home to consider their chatty ways. I recognise no authority in this world and ancestor birds accompany me on that same alien cartography.

Black Mariah

When they come to get you, that is, to take you for that joy ride, for that last long sentence into the night remember when it was not so, when laughter was spry and not a commentary: they will search for you in that castle, all geared up for some sort of WWIII because you know it's coming don't you, that scourge of the word: full stops make no sense, commas a half sneer on the court of the page and then it will be all over red rover red rover red rover – please do not revive me on this peninsula, this erudite quote on the page of *was soll es bedeuten* – you just know the full stop is right around that terrible corner, the wind will suddenly stop, the birds will go wild and screech into destiny and all the cows will suddenly turn and face east in expectation, and like them, you will finally know about end-things, its grip on the mother tongue, your heart stretching to take it all in, but that black Mariah is coming, you know that don't you: no castles, no ramparts, blown up bridges or vast stretches of land mines can stop them.

War

Thank you cloud and clod for
the broken step   the cranked car
Orange tables in the Synagogue
the smite across the sky

He delivers his mote like a log in his eye
heroes all dead everyone   he is a gendarme
a legionnaire   a crying babe

We lap the bowl and think we have it made
tourists in a jungle of marching fire ants
leaping cane toads   We are observers of a country
where the spleen is split and I come out of the operation
like a landed guppy

The machinery of being

The machinations of men (you never hear of women)
what metal they're made of
    models of behaviour
    well-oiled plans   steely eyed
    you crash for the night
    steel yourself for battle
squeaky wheel gets the oil
another cog   the wheels of justice
in the pipeline   our hopes and dreams
the taste of metal on the tongue
crosswires of hope and hate
it just does not compute   those pawns in the game
hardwired, transfixed   sliding door moments
she's as hard as nails   step on it, gun it
I am fenced in   unretractable   flying high
fractured, fragmented   cold as steel, he blows his lid
mind like a steel trap, she's triggered, boxed in
he's at the wheel

Great waves of Hokusai San

Into the void, or next door   a baby cries
I yell, scream, inside   it's all gotten too much (the world
I mean) and I'm looking for emptiness or completeness or
something   She stretches   Babinski reflex
fingers grasping

In this, my Autumn home, I stretch too but my grasping
comes to naught   sometimes I receive a gift
Sometimes, nothing

I pick the child up, give her comfort, human touch
if she is not to die, bereft of connection, to us all

Pick yourself up, get on with it
bring it home, whatever it is
that smiling triumph over the everyday
just as now the child must do, will do

Reach out you mangy mut
the world waits for nothing but
the great waves will come

Merry-go-round

The wind blows to the south, and goes round and round to the north:
round and round goes the wind, and the wind returns to its going around.

Ecclesiastes 1: 6

Return again   don't just return me to the store
buy me outright   own me, own your own shit, eat bread this day
don't just break it: the rat-wheel   are we not all prime suspects
are we not viable   our fields fertile with cash?
Cows, ploughed into millions of acres of virgin jungle
we all want our piece of the hamburger-pie

It is said there is some sort of slippery slope, uphill and down
again again again   Take the strain great Sisyphus and your stone
we step into the stream and are changed and yet we are again

Eat me, consume me   mighty bitcoin
allure me with your glimmer your call-girl cry
out to the wilderness, until round and round
like a merry-go-round   It seems we are no longer affordable

Pave the Way

A voice cries: 'In the wilderness prepare the way of the Lord,
make straight in the desert a highway for our God.'

Isaiah 40: 3

Did not someone, some centenary ago times a plenty
rightly write   a voice, out there, in the ether, on the wire

Was it not downloaded some time ago, say, to make a beeline
correct the road which we roughed out in the bush
along a lonely coastal edge through thickets of she-oaks
spinifex and banksias

Did not that Primary Voice command us, lay it down straight
upon a stony desert highway   even in that red, red dirt
leave lay your bleached bones along the side of the road
for the carrion, ants, and flies to pick clean

Join the dots if you must   East to West, South and
in some Northern Kapok fields   Draw the Linear
be my surveyor with your sure eye
pave the Way wanderer and do not waver

Rule of God

Turn away thy reproach which I dread: for thy ordinances are good.
Behold, I long for thy precepts: in thy righteousness give me life!

Ps 119: 39

Lay your orders down, over the peeling tree, over errant blades of grass, the melting stone   Sun sets down Bayview Road, the Bay whale-blue: set your statutes, Lord, over my wanderings – my blank musings: perhaps ordinance shelters my fraying mind and on afternoons such as this, sun-suppurated, bird-songed and wind-wisped as gums flood their feathery leaves   Let me understand the way of the ant-warrior and share its burden: march on, march on good soldier, finish your dutiful step and lift, make your colony strong   give me a hint, lay it on me   rule of God.

Psalm 105

It is enough to remember, the rain of frogs and blood, to contemplate the days in decline: water rises, water rations and others play with lives forgotten, unrecorded in towns long unknown.

It is enough to remember heroes, myths signs, scrawled on dunny walls: a child cries after she drops her ice cream, the street thrums with through traffic: am I the only one – I think not – to notice burnt offerings, symbols of children.

In the steps of Chief Joseph of the Nez Perce

Cast the Tarot   throw the I Ching
who in their right mind would want to live in the bore of
life's bling   Put me under the granite in Glinton's graveyard
somewhere near there with John Clare or in Northborough with
Lucia Joyce and their madnesses

Lay my bones under the ground in the *Cemitero Acattolico* with
John Keats   Ask the Oracle all you need to know and
forgo tepid and staid book knowledge   rather skew me with
your razor incendiary-words while I wait for Godot

Raise me a storm tempest and capsize my Jack *de* Crow dinghy
Break me a breach and seal my lips forever rather than death by article
letters wasted in the vast halls of nothing   dust-decayed on the shelves
at Cambridge or Oxford   rather let me die with Ramanujan and
his formulae garnered from his goddess Lakshmi who will one day
solve the riddle of the Black Hole and the event horizon

Grow me into the gravelly hills around this desert-coast city and

if all else fails, bury my heart with the murdered souls at Wounded Knee

unfit though I am   Scatter my ashes at Pinjarra with the Binjareb

whose bones are washed in the Murray River still

I will tag along with Chief Joseph and his lost tribe

and scribe my nothingness in the Dakota hills   let my words

die with me there

I, John Clare

They say he turned mad at the end of his days and
if that's true I'm happy to be numbered there with him
to wander in the shadow of madness' well loaded message and
the pithiness it brings: my own Epping Forest looms before me
my Hertfordshire and Petersborough
my own Orison pock marked by weird words, neologisms,
strange vernacular that seems to pressure and interrupt:
time   place   orientation   I am in constant remission

I do not wish to mock the poet's state, his pain
I do not wish to assume some false mantle
only to say that my ramblings have led me on strange journeys
apple picking   chefing   scything
I too am an itinerant remembering lost love relishing
the newly found   reeling   regaling   reaping

If these are the demon's markers then let me drink deep the draft
let me drown in its embers: succumb to the siren's song

I wanted to say, there's so much I want to do, to write, to remember to build on the road from me to you

there's a forest of undone things I want to plant

a series of armies I want to lead across rivers of sweat

a desert of unspoken thoughts to cross: a collected works to read

But I cannot   this day's not long enough

mountains have crumbled, glaciers dried up

last month we lost forty percent of the polar cap

several species of butterfly have disappeared   bees are dying

I have to find my wife again, Mary who, they say, has died long ago

but they have a nice place for me to stay in Epping Forest Asylum

Meet you at the Opus 109

After the deluge, conversations deep into the Black Forest and
we arranged our next meeting at the Opus 109
the e-major sonata to be precise   We had made detailed plans
It was to be in Edinburgh   on my 70th birthday
Much had been digested the last time we were there
perhaps lifetimes even
the squaring off of old debts, plenty of platitudes, evil designs on
our enemies, renewed vows of love for those we held dear
Life is a boat with all its loaded metaphors

we ended up on the rocks, sailing into stormy winds,
sunny days, took anchor, took refuge, held our course,
rerouted the trip, sailed the high seas, had our highs and lows
set a new course, lived our life according to and under the stars
some days in the doldrums when we really had nothing to do
and boredom was the bay in which we were shored up

I told him that it was near the Opus 109 that I wanted it to happen
I get it, but the pace was beyond me   Play it *prestissimo* they said and
I was immediately off key, thrown   There were depths, deviations

but the improv was what got to me and if I die there

in that sleet-grey city of granite and greatness

say of a pulmonary embolism or

some other such weird death please make sure it is there

somewhere near or around the Opus 109

Liminal

There exists, between the realm of angels & kingdoms of men, another race altogether. Some here, the likes of Hesiod and Enoch, have recognised: those wanderers & recorded them as Watchers. They were then, as they remain, the deceivers or, more to the point, deceive lings because, as with many sent by the gods, they had no idea what they were getting into. Simply more play for cruelty, love and lust.

•

Let's go somewhere, he says.

Where? She asks.

I don't care – anywhere.

What do you want to do?

Anything.

& they did. They tasted prickly pear: they rode elevators to the 50th floor just to look over the city through the city-to-floor window from the bathroom: they felt sea-spray splash up over the sprawling basalt rocks down at the end of the groyne.

& they loved, like children, but it couldn't last & at the end, when all the tears were drained from them, they felt angry, betrayed: by whom? By what?

•

The angels, they coax, entice, invite, call & we, all too easily seduced, attempt to heed the call, to approach that upper Kingdom, as if it were actually possible. We proceed to build up that hope & call it by many names like Camelot, Babel, Rome: all Heavenly, all Dust as if what goes up must

come down. America calls us, like a Cumulus Nimbus hung in a crying blue sky.

•

Lead us up that spiral stairway into the Ninth, unknown circle of Dante's Hell & the crashing waves would carry us onto the crushed sand to find there, on the shore, the sweet edge of that plate which we lick like kids. Something's missing. Just out of reach, always at finger-tip edge to finger-tip, singing out like buildings tumbling down into the Sea. Never quite there. Like Angels towards the dry dirt, not quite or, she, standing upon the bridge looking skywards like a plea looking downwards like inevitability & somewhere in-between another race we cannot conceive but somehow sent to deceive. They, so remote & their celestial music, but I feel the wind salty through my fingers & the graining waves through my toes: it is not in vain this edge, this liminal & strophed day.

Anywhere

Non-ownership in the unpropitious moment and perhaps even inauspicious · this loss · this very conspicuous lack · shades, sheds, rivers, creeks, cricked crickets and other arthropods · there go I brother · spineless and craggy · arthritic, nebulous, a no where man – no point of view · with no qualities · he who does not listen · making no plans

Mornings flow like lava · wash over me like unleashed and unconstrained histories · myths of my own making · no ownership here, no music making will salve this skin · but sleep again and up over again · Here, this place, there, it does not matter – anywhere · bring me comfort in that afternoon tea as day runs like the ticking clock · Hurt me again, amor fati · do your best, little beast · I do love you awful thing, acrimonious Nacirema · nacrimonious neologism · This is what is has come to · awash in unknown numbers, neuros, nefarious undoings and redoings · Truth: the hard thought of a prawn

Another entirely different road

Crows in broken formation across the sky-gris
Below them, the church   Our Lady of Lourdes
square towered against the dark-light morning
I stand waiting on High Road
notice pulled shades of the Dentist's room
on the lower floor of the tenancy
Its name draws me like some sort of Scottish manor
like out of some Vincent Price movie
Dunkeld   It is apt here as the early tram rattles by
as I board, jacket-scarved, cold-pressed
Almost nostalgic this kind of displacement
Lourdes, Dunkeld like a memory of a home
or some spiritual journey
but I have left behind another, entirely different road,
gravell'd   valley'd where the air was bright and full sunned
when I was a kid crystal brook cackling
crows   less auspicious, less murderous

Self-revealed

Body disembodied   feet touch the ground   eyes might meet singular paths this freshwater morning   Who is this self not here yet an awaiting revelation of self to self   in conversation with friends not known till   death birth hails a revealing smile, tear   Not now, yet, anchoring illness and joy   Beguiling story on the screen, on paper We arise, a surface not here but only when a glance from a stranger or vacant stare and then, that dirty Da'esh image   a beheading   a young man living   here, now and not   I am then and hence dislocated   My feet still touch the ground but they are on their own Vacant stare into nowhere and someone's son, brother, father is gone: a bloody summons   the day is self-revealed yet self is not   still the image remains

Found (*ad honorem Ross Seaton*)

… he pushed his wheelbarrow along Stirling Highway making his daily journey toward the ocean.

… his own man, a Don Quixote with his wheelbarrow Rocinante setting out each day to find meaning in the world.

On Saturday 23 May, when we had planned to pick up our certificates of flu injection, in preparation for our visit, Kevin rang. He informed me that Ross had died. It was a shock and a surprise.

… he searched for some underlying meaning that would make sense of the universe. It was a pursuit that gradually filled his waking hours. And he walked, he walked a lot. Every day he set off to the beach or the river …

it was a journey of discovery, full of information that needed to be computed and processed. License plate numbers, receipts, and randomly sourced codes were clues to some overarching algorithm that would somehow explain the anomalies of this phenomenal world.

Life is a fiction a drama that demands continuous creation no matter the apparent cost.

Each trip was a quest for materials to make art … First in a wheelbarrow, then a series of discarded prams he renovated for purpose, Ross would embark each day down Bulimba Road to Stirling Highway, then on towards Cottesloe or Fremantle, sometimes making it to the ocean for an invigorating swim, sometimes ... at the beach drawing, writing notes or staring out to sea.

Stones and shells stained with blue paint at Sandtrax ...

Ross stayed in the sleepout till 1998, when it became so packed with paintings, drawings and books that he was forced to move into the laundry to sleep. There — his head under the sink his long legs and curved back arched toward the door — for a further fourteen years.

Do whatever it takes! Life should be tough, beyond ordinary endurance.

Clearly ... some paintings were more significant than others.

'It's the Force,' he whispered one day ... 'The Force?'
'It's important, but later, I'll tell you later,'

There is a pattern to be found if one looks long enough... There is some localised pattern in any random arrangement. Therefore, this is enough to create a work of art .

---

*A poem found in *Walking Man: Ross Seaton*. By Ted Snell. All words in this poem belong to Ted who has kindly and generously leant them to me to rearrange. Italics quoted directly from Ross Seaton.

Calvary (*after the movie*)

If a man told you to meet with him even with his spoken intention of shooting you, would you still go? Would you have completed your contrition? Would your affairs be in order? Would you take back those hurtful things you said or did or thought? Where would the first place be where you would look for forgiveness and who would you ask for it? Would you search for the origins of your angry, unthinking, hurtful self? How deep would you be prepared to dig on that day of your proposed demise? Or would you run? Relinquish the self that would kneel on that beach and take the bullet like a man?

Anaphora

As winds are we born   or we might ask
unto wherein are we thrown

I thought I said enough … enough, no more!
Regret over such things   such things!

The story   our story   our personal narrative
sad mad glad or bad
of which we can do nothing   nix   nada   nyet
kein   absolutely zero
to repeat   to go back to   where one was
to revisit   retreat   retrieve

It bodes no one well   no good to do so
and yet   yet we are often asked to do just that
     where are you from   our roots, your background
country of origin   what happened?

We cannot evade the curious, the nosy   yet this is not always

Sometimes honest inquiries trying to connect   perhaps
trying to reach out ... to touch   you   in the right way
a meaningful, enriching, enlivening way that can make you
feel loved   I never even heard that word
even though they, you   somehow   exactly do know
that they, your loved ones, did indeed
love you

Memory Incinerates

Fragile as dark snow, cinders of memory. If one could only
rescind, go back, would I? Would I change one milli metre
of any of it? The rash word, the unleashed wound, the escaped
clause of my body exposed to the hills, along the Darling lapis edge.
Take these damn fingers, these shoulders, this migraine neck and
return me to yonder for that one-more-glimpse.

Freshwater creeks that still trickle, there beyond Hovea,
Sawyers Valley, Mahogany Creek, down the Helena River
valley where we clattered and clambered: kids like mountain goats
along those washed-out clay firebreaks, down, down to the river.
Irascible bush, zephyr-cooled over pool's edges bush-cutting
me an image that will not rest and lives on like a fire to this day.
Run – run rabbit, run it off, chill that scribbled mind and let it flow
like the creeks, rivulets into the bush there to scribe yourself always.

Gleaming wears out the gaze

Bush creeks through the back end of Mundaring Weir – look there - where? I missed it. The child - imagination in overdrive: ferns, stones, trickling clearest water over broken logs, crags and reeds, impish spirits. Invisible kingdoms. Invisible fathers, gone off with the fairy king, out on the white water, rafting where? Children play like dolphins, and I also remember, Ross, that we fathers too play. Jarrahs, Marri, Blackboys trails leading to the never-never and return. God's Jewels – mist hangs in the bush like sparkling diamonds, mystery dew drops, and a thousand webs reveal themselves suddenly in the frosty morning. We laugh as the echidna trundles its way up the bushy driveway and snakes hang lazily in the summer sun across the rocks around the fishpond in the back yard. Did we know? Anything? Years fly by like ancient pterodactyls piercing the world with arrow-shrieks of certainty. They died out as we too will in our own days. Did we know?

Corrode away

With one hand, wax on, the mirage begins, and we, drawn in like moths, like flies into what? The canker of sweet things, broken warnings falling like so many stone-stars scattered along gravel roads; but where were they, those surreptitious caveats? I searched and searched in the creeks of the valleys, the twigged pathways of the bush, on the road to Mundaring to get clobbered there by kismet, the bauxite of the place and its fatal signs leading to the wider beyond of the wheat-belt that did no one no good in this blessed West where, it is said, people go to die. Corrode my rusty corrugated, my deadly water tank from which I drank how many dead frogs and various decaying metals; and yet, here I stand like some sort of shibboleth to those who come after me; where is he, that invisible man? Felled between the stone edges in a rose garden where you weeded weekend after fucking weekend, slave labourers got treated better, but *Arbeit macht frei*, and so it goes, corrode away my little beauty, corrode away ....

Water under the bridge (*after Lucy Ellmann*)

… how I don't want this to be a memory thing · rather a you-had-to-be-there kind of thing · to feel the Pemberton breeze blowing through the dusk bush, to taste that sumptuous brown trout you just caught · trout, tout, face-about, snout, roast pig · and how I shouldn't say that in these vegan times, roast pig I mean · and how that trout thing was when my child was just born, that was back then, and how, today, I was at my childhood friend's funeral and listened to his grown children's eulogies · how he was only two years older than me and how his wife of forty two years died two years ago and their kid's kids will not know grandparents · paring, faring, staring into the gathered crowd of mourners · talking about the things we first-gen Australian-Austrians did as kids and how that really was a remembering thing ? and how we all seemed to have lost track of each other over the years · and how sad it is to think that was over how-many years ago I had last seen them only to watch now as they slide the coffin into that weird ante-room where they will 'take care of you', like in Evelyn Waugh's *The Loved One* and how o-so-pure that book was · but how not so pure it all is out here, outside the purifying fires of the crematorium · and us kids, the things we got up to and how, brown cow, dig that plough, it's all water under the bridge now

Seemliness

Saturday night
could be any Old Town   it is here
out there on the Leach highway
usually around 9pm-ish they begin
those screaming banshee sirens   Death, life
police, ambulances
they continue and even more distantly
like a screaming Indian Ocean high velocity wind
the sirens as if they're coaxing each other
the hoons, crooks, bad guys, good guys   whatever
giving a fecund chase that will soon end
in some cacophony of dies when new generations
have given up on wanting what's real
with no templates surviving to show what might be
isn't that what happens all the time? Apparently, she says
as she continues with her drawing   On TV the movie
is about a nation winning freedom from tyrants
only to become so themselves

it's all about patriots   the sirens will always be
have always been   Even in the shrieks they seduce us still
as did Odysseus' ships of the night   up is down
here is yonder   All I hear is crickets
there is a silence in this coast town   this Indian sea
into the night east West North South   The siren call
it lets me know and lets me know and perhaps
it is a wake-up   Truth, apparently, as she says
is not as it seems

languageslips

I

The aroma of strings falling like manna over red dunes.

Twenty-nine diadems gone: floating in sounds of bare winter trees.

The heat of her heart there in my soup, there on the screen of rankling stone and branch. The chorus of blue and emerald-green eaten like rust.

She broke it to me that her feet were glue to the earth and

the crashing waves around her head sonorous: hair tousled, the evening quenched, stars dusted and done and slept like a tractor ploughing the heavens in search of kingdoms relinquished, driven

like an earn full of oxen.

Bring me my wages so that I can alleviate

the masses, take them through snowfields, raise corn and

write sonata after sonata. This sound, this breath like tungsten

all around in the air of my retirement. Broken

teeth, harps, tremors there, in the valley across from the oceans

of larch, ash and oak.

Send me home again. Let me cook up a French soup for you and

we can eat Zen all day long. We belong under fingernails:

we build sunshine over a backstreet hidden from fading eyes.

II

In this moment, the white-green of the rising and already tall, yet still sapling, birch and beyond it the snow-grey of sky and there too the cross beams of the telephone post over-reaching the crossroads as Indian Mina birds fly like new conquerors and cars crenellate the cold asphalt.

'Sweet as …' echoes from the porch across the street as kids waltz their way to important destinations with an urgency that could start a war: it is cold, but not enough as the wind brings news of what's to come. I listen as I have no option, the roses giving their Autumn last and the moment, like a hexagon flake, drifts and melts into the waiting earth.

III

The sound of wash-up along the channel at night

like a red corvette cruising through the Midlands on brown-dusty days up into Launceston · the Tamar breathes the valley with lavender but still a zero-sound · Still the hollow mountains, drifting coasts and sea that brushes and soughs and reaches · reaches, but can no longer touch · simply sedges, pathways, points to somewhere where coordinates are lost or otherwise meaningless

Schist breaks, knurls, crumbs its clumsy sound-way back under and over the salty waves cracking the timeless code of these dunes · The sifting sweep holds the key if only we could un-blind our face, untwine our feet · break through our thighs and shins and walk upright again as the people once did to watch wonderingly over lapping waves, coves and bays

IV

Plovers in the nearby park · did they make the grass on which they stand and through which they sift, or the worms and insects which are hidden · a banquet table · I do not own even my next minute and the short-lived clouds diminish my intrigue and plans

I step into the river and I am different, as Heraclitus said I would be · perhaps baptised as the Greeks · parrots and thrushes in the pink-flowered gums that line this street show me up and screech and flee at the sight of me · I labour, look to others for coin and cover · stumble onto the road, my asphalt, my sure step · tomorrow is dust and a bunch of parsley and my tongue, dry in a climate of change, it stitches to the roof of my mouth and I am dumb (as Blake said)

V

Bring the night
devoid of rainy light and listen
to the pitting on the roof   sunrise disappeared
long ago and into the vagueness of days
I speak a kind of deafness

It's not hard to see such things
just as it's not hard to sail through Thursday, Friday and
forever when the only things you have to concern yourself
with are questions about how long these hours are
how many more semi clefs on this bridge of sound
that becomes a blip that becomes a song on day's horizon

VI

Under today's grey skies   under any other name
draw the line at the doorway where salesgirls wait
unknowing   The doors remain open
use them if you must, it's a two-way street
the commerce of breads salads and some varieties
of salvation awaits them, those kids in the waiting lines

Slip in, out, along
Your divorce last week was the last straw
but the super will continue to kick in

How many more varieties of bread?

You take one with the LOT and
outside the sleet-grey sky suggests it's probably gonna
be perfect up on the mountains for skiing

VII

Carapace of cracked branch, twig node and nodule around and through this tiled house-sea · like a crag of winter's nests, fogged and forgotten · all I see are splinter and frore · Chimney stacks poking through · wires teleport good news, tragedy · streets, traffic under foreign skies · Asphalt awaits my steps towards shops and the commerce of loveliness · sadness deep-cuts tendons, arteries · cuts my eyes and my brow

Gutters overflow reluctantly · rust, my map · fists full of uselessness · breaking our feet on stones of anticipation · our sons and daughters inherit only to lash out once more · freeing up ancestors, binding descendants chaining us to the wheel · Turn turn like the wheeling gull, broken-footed over a sea of riches · we eat stew, sing slated roof tops, revel in the bend of bough · Another day in the suburbs

VIII

Bright moon concealing egrets · they fly, those long birds, around the crown of the moon, around the world · reach me through the air which I heavily breathe · in · out · Moon, egrets and I · united in breath, in the glance over ones shoulder · Did I know this would be a journey · this father-son regret life?

The moon shines and by flying egrets hidden like snow in a silver bowl · I see no reflection · Him, I we, us · this is the story of a Johnny rotten · long ago, but not forgotten · this is the story of a forgiving grace that sheds its clear light and of remembrance in a child's trace.

IX

Under the sun, the sway of light glistens · let me know if this is not so · Only yesterday the winter-cold, only last term the clouds from off the mountains snow-grey and biting to the bone · so tell me now if the sun don't shine and I'll head off · My skin finds some colour again · my bald pate browns up · *times are changing, things have changed* · Let the vibe over the Bass Clef display the way, guide the notes · the high and middle · let the diatonic scale C tickle my ribs ·

This much I know, now, that up is down, round is a square · Die, live, cry and by the by over the hill and far away · In my kitchen the soup waits, pandemics come and go, vaccines may or may not avert the decimation of my friends · But the sun still holds ground and sky, and I · We have faced all these things and next term the leaves fall from trees once again · Tomorrow I am not, and then again, it's not up to me to say

X

Mercury-sand time slips like a silent sibilant creature
Through my eyes · my hair · down my throat

My voice croaks · Is suddenly clear
The stars seem brighter today
Tomorrow they are near again

I will lose all perspective and restraint
Perhaps become a petulant teenage poet
At the foot of Parnassus and tug at the beards of the greats

Break open the gates · let the vandals in
Savage gods play · ancient codes crumble like sand pies and
I will eat them humbly again yesterday and tomorrow
Gladly again like some sort of *Amor Fati*

XI

If we could see – me, us, them – what would we see? A hanging variegated ivy, a rabbit's foot fern, dishevelled bookcase, game of Scrabble. Through the wide window a passionfruit in the backyard growing wild: distant cloud-striae. Salmon have died for this, bike riders given their lycra best in large packs on Saturday mornings down Beach Road along the Bay, past Brighton, Hampton, Sandringham   the sweep of flat water, turquoise.

Perhaps if god could give His fourth finger for this we'd be undone, cardiac-arrested in some ED, wake up, look that nurse in the eye and know we are done for: our vocation lost, everything we believed in retrenched, we'd know that yesterday wouldn't mean a thing.

If we could see us. Me. Pegged, like a small-winged bird, a fractured animal, a pieced-together hybrid, a new universe would unfold, secret codes cracked: surgery will definitely be in order. It is dark: the fly in the room, like the wind outside, persistent. Maybe tomorrow I'll swat it into infinity. I have seen this before and before that.

XII

Yonder in the chilled outside it darkens. The low hum of autumn leaves either browns or disappears completely. The old guy, across the road, still sits in the cold, twilight verandah, radio blaring loud as ever. The young couple next door to him in the depths of toddler child, early years and all that young love entails such as: the intolerable weight of water, the heavy hand of familiarity, the blood hound of undeniability, the inevitability of wear and tear.

If I was to tell them the truth, that there is no train in the station, so don't bother waiting: that no one will come and hug them when the terrible day arrives, and they will melt into the sand of the unknowable.

Perhaps salve them in talk of *tomorrow is another day*, that, in fact, the hand that feeds will never withdraw and that it is worth it after all: that the world really does care and after autumn comes winter, yes, but then spring and summer once again.

XIII

Outside, in the garden, the birch tree it did grow · 'twas an everwhirling wind wound its leaves hither and thither and *a wild cat did growl* · 'Twas ever so, the meandering I mean, people of every cut and cloth

Go steady – do not cry · carts bumbling along, and there, that old man by the wayside falls, a heap of bones and rye · There go I · The wind soughs softly now · even it trembles and sends a clarion call into the world: one more is down, one less to feed, to clothe to care for or about · Sun recovers, sends another flare · fare thee old man – did you die alone · did the crows come and pick your eyes, the dog lick your festering and howl ? Did the moon that night wane or wax

In the distance, the trees on the hilltop, that dark church, the collapsing crumbling cemetery stones · This decade disappears, as with the dodo birds whom they deliciously ate and then no more · Do not cry old man, they'll not hear you · all your children are dead and there is no one to mourn you

XIV

Pour all yourself into me Beethoven, roll over, let me die impaled upon any one of your sonatas, yours or Dvořák and your *Forget-Me-Not Polka* on any given ... rain over me private beings, hidden discursive: did someone say Beautiful and then die?

O Mars unhitch me on the way there to your red realms, drill me into the core of your dusty surface and inter me there: like Wounded Heart teach me your solfege: Do Re Mi Fa Sol La Ti Do: Who, ever has played a note, one single minim or semi-breve worthy of the effort?

... lay me over your staff. If I am blind-deaf, let me taste the air of your distant planet because tomorrow we are no more: the sun will shine its brightest, the spheres will let us know all about it and hope will be no more: until then let me spell that word for you, spill that music: pour yourself, maestro, into me, let me dream big things and listen to the music once more.

XV

Sandwiches   britches bitches stiches
we find ourselves in *regardez*
take note, ephebe
always   always, bread buns Turkish pita Lebanese
sour   dough sloughs slow broth bro
the slippage   *la langue*   *die Sprache*

Speech-net in which we are webbed stabbed trenched
whereon we are benched bagged nabbed
and which we attempt to breach
britches bitches stitches

XVI

The negotiations of the bending bough, soft, soft, in the hard breeze · a cinereous glare beyond and between these deliberate branches and a faint falling air to the footpath below · the street – emptyish · the tone - pregnant · sometimes like the young mums and dads that cruise this part of town, like they are carting something important, wonderful or just going for a hurried walk keeping trim perhaps, the babe bored or restless

Rustling leaves tell me otherwise, that the sky between them and me is kind of sacred or something, no matter the arbitrary nature of this urban street, the vicissitudes of these neighbourhoods on any other day · the sound of the odd motorbike, whirring · the slight chatter in the house next door as they finish the painting · Stop this now, this nonsense of greened fences, community shrub and tasteless walkways, don't the gods have some say in this · relegate me to the museum of 'too much', or the gallery of 'not enough' or even the corporate headquarters of 'when will this glory end'

Babbling children manifest the dance of tomorrow, the bread of today and the impasse of yesterday · the babe in the carriage looks up at the swaying branches, heavy with too many seasons and sees its days mounting in an ever-inciting moment

XVII

Breathe the air effervescent · times eternal youth and light · and I bright as a new-born button sitting on my mother's lap waiting to be sewn · It is days of light and wonder · did I cover all the bases · am I ready for the coming thud of winter and out there along the waysides, roads and various laneways and avenues · Am I ready for Damocles · for crunch time · relinquished of my duty, beholden to no-one and nothing? · On this rock under the vacuum sky, sealed and delivered subject to the rains of cosmos – comets, solar flares and such like imaginations · Breach the seal I say and undo pianos, cats, bottle brushes · wash me of my sins, regale me with tales of heroes and heroines · Bathe me in glorious times gone by and I will crash the gates · Play the scornful and cry like a newborn, it is time for something I have not heard of before · a new season on the edge of the world · time to yonder into the paddocks on the other side · and if I fall, if I fail like a bastard, then so be it

XVIII

You sent me three photos:
an ochre casa, the kid in her dad's uniform, the line-up
of sauces: mustard, ranch, mayo, hot, tomato seemingly endless

The child looks like a shrivelled old man
the casa like a place I would love to live, for a while at least
God knows I've lived in my share of places across this country
and come to love Paul Kelly's latest offering *Sleep, sleep*
while you count your sheep

The sauces spoke to me loud and clear
how we love to smother things with other things
bury the tasteless, perhaps unpalatable things, maybe like truths
or something   Things happen we don't want to know

XIX

Sing the song sister, unleash that wretched groan, the dog in our neighbour's backyard, she lets us know, howling like lost hound at an unseen moon which will come out tonight and flood me with illuminated and murky truths, half-truths, outright lies. Be my werewolf, my dingo guide in this fearful land: we tread onto tightropes that hardly fit on the sole of the foot: sway with the swing of it, remember, don't remember, make shit up: Christ if it was left to us, we'd be our own myths, our own made-up monsters, mermaids, meth addicts. We slip in, out like homeless mothers at the shelters: social workers attempt to steer us in the right direction, yet we refuse, refute, elude, elide the cold light of day facts of the matter: the so-called truth. Life is music and let no archetypal Mr Jones tell you any different.

XX

So here is how it ends this looking ·skywards ·half-eaten
moon crust soft in its milkiness and cuspiness ·outline
of the fiddle-leaf tree crisp, like a lost continent in a sea of blue

Urban hew of brick cutters, gurgling magpies,
child-chatter ·breeze across my forehead ·an old lady
and her dog·butterfly that flits ·bee that blusterly buzzes ·
diosma that bleeds its dried grass green ·cars that rumble

I am back on the dozy deck in front of the house ·Look up
up up and absorb this mirage ·this could-all-end-tomorrow
as it has for others already ·Skywards my gaze and make more
pictures in my ears ·in my nose ·on my fingers ·in my eyes

WATERS OF THE HEART

When I was young

When I was still young, before I went on my travels,
I sought wisdom openly in my prayer. Before the temple I asked
for her, and I will search for her till the last.

                                    Sirach 51: 13 – 14

I did many stupid things when I was young
blame the neuro wiring   blame the decades and the times
maybe that's just what kids do: stupid stuff, but I did travel
 my brain could not sit still then

nor my feet nor my stomach and the fruits of the earth
were my prayer for the day, the bread I broke and the wine
down that dusty Tasmanian road or two I slurried

People came and went   friends, enemies, Romans
like fresh cut grass flashed before a yearling in pasture
It was an enough-life   rain, heat, fences, scorching skies
clouds, bush, gravel-road days till I came before the temple
of your home   domesticity and all that   where I knelt

like a broken pony and worshipped at the Gate of Her

I kissed your deep, dark hair   I kowtowed to your glorious gift, eating the fruit that only you brought me

We were both young then, we did foolish and unspeakable things

you, utterly unkeepable, and by my side still

Hard marrow

Leaven this cob · rise the flour · take great chunks
and dip them in oil which pours from a hillside crevice or
runs unseen around granulated bends · bake the moment, the fable
or the myth or other literature · unhinge me in this infernal and leaf
your way through the book of me

What will you find? Hard marrow, cooling blood, blistering and bile
  that needs tempering soothed on the balm of some nirvana home-made
  unction blessed by a local bone pointer or far away *brujo*

Heart

Thou hast opened my heart for thy understanding
My heart murmurs ... and my heart melts like wax
because of iniquity and sin ...
    The Thanksgiving Hymns, Qumran Hymn XXII

Send in the clouds, snow, and ice · heart of mine
A wide range on this southern horizon where the kitchen is warm
eggs and chorizo freckled in the frying pan · There are other duties
to distract, to peel my eyes for this day · A crumbled monastery
far far away on a Dead Sea

Is this day not enough · parrots gambolling the gums all around ·
Perhaps hearts do melt ? they are tiny like a little wren and,
crushed once, can they ever truly bounce back · Look to the beyond
there over the zigzag skyline to a wider sea that breathes for us all

forget me, honey

call my lips a parchment upon
which inadequate words engrave
witness this, my forgotten home, my body
long abandoned by bees · a sinewed, blooded place ·
snow has no right here · cinders fly like everyday rain
and oranges sweetly explode · Perhaps forget me, honey
my permanent residence · is this the best we can do · witnessed
by distant, glimmer · suns that lustre us · Rearrange my hair
with your veracious fingers · drown me in your succulent
nectar · relegate me in your honesty and there I
a frayed broken rope

Nearing

Approach and it distances   they
... *make the world go away* ...*
But there it is   they   still
Bring the tea darling   let's set the table, you and I
she said

O so close   sitting nearby and she, they, might as well be
on Andromeda   That's how together we can be
today over breakfast, there in the car or
at the movies   these days, one blink away

Write me a libretto will you
work me up a thesis on these moments   gems
to be strung like glass beads
see how nearly they sit to each other

Wire me the money will you when you get there
at the edge of that desert, send me a note

I will be waiting   as always

* *Make the world go away as sung by Elvis*

Refurbish

Render unto them, they say   it says
the book that is ...

An empty bottle   what's it got
O bring me my pills

Indictments, inducements are my calling
Make over, do over   renovate me
this useless vessel, empty carcase   broken transom

There is cruelty around the corner
The sofa needs attention, the garden needs weeding
where it is we are all going
blind folded or not

They say my children will thank me

Letters to Milena

Dear Milena, Franz K sits for you naked
on his deck chair at the Pension Ottoburg
he writes of lizards and semi-comatose beetles, cockroaches.
All the voices of the prophets are alive for you

in the *breath of your eyes*, Milena. His days, short
as his poisoned breath: the air at his Pension is clear
forgive him Milena for he is weak as a child-prophet.
His race is numbered as the stars above. *Škatule Škatule* he plays.

He falters, falls down, lies on the ground and he can
no longer listen to your terrible voice and all it tells of blood
race and lungs. You die in the camps.
At least his tuberculosis saved him from that.

Letters to Ophelia Queiroz

Terrible Baby he writes to his love
Pessoa the poet with many names who does not exist
whose sad and solitary literary life ends in a quiet,
leafy Rua and who died countless times
so many non-suicides
Everyone imaginable inside him was alive till one day
too young he is dead of an alcoholic's liver

Dear naughty little baby he scribbles hastily on an unused
office invoice where he works as a non-existent translator
writing thousands upon thousands of pages of words that
could halt a storm and bring a mythical King back to life
Sebastião I of Portugal, the Hidden one   *Encobertoa*
Sebastian   myth-king and Saviour

Angel baby   the poet writes to his little Ibis, his quiet bird
disconsolate in her own office not far from his, she loves him
We will get married soon, she implores him her *nininho* Fernando
she writes to all of him   his many selves, all of them

none of whom could commit to her even as he promises

to eat her lips, her kisses

My little wasp he lures her, conjures into being his literary lair

there across from the Cascais Station there in a local streetcar

they play with great fidelity their 1920's love game

she will hold onto his many love letters written to be read by who?

Only her or his imagined other selves

My dear sweet baby he calls her

love is fleeting like a letter scribbled on the back

of a receipt from a lonely man who does not know he is the one

who has not written to her   He scribes from the prison

of himself   Prisoner Zero as his pancreas goes up in flames

Dearest Ophelia   the truth of it is I have my life's work

to attend   not that half of it will be finished before I end

not long from now and you will go on to marry and have children

I will rest (or not) in disquietude and join my others waiting

patiently on the shore of their future King

Sweet Ibis   Terrible wasp   Sweet darling Ophelia

do not blame me for them who I am

even when you can see that I am not and never was

Fernando Pessoa † 1935

Ophelia Queiroz † 1991

Flowers of the mouth (*after Baudelaire*)

Torment me sweet, horrible, torturous flower
break this easy façade   the biblical bluster
Coitus your secrets in me, leave nothing unsaid or undone
plant your lips upon mine

Hit me while the sun shines, caress me with your sharp claws
curve ball   undo my illusions, my wafty habits and disingenuous
ways   instead, make me real into your world
make me bleed

Breach these obsessions
sink those flowery teeth into this heart
do what you must do and be on your way where I can't follow
then turn and beckon me to come

Thirty-seven summers have passed and I am still not
onto to your wily ways   I still live in a daydream where
we met   You promised me nothing, but delivered everything
Hurt me bad, you bad, bad girl

take this disgusting flower from my mouth

Plant your lips on mine   bite them till they bleed

Fallen guy

She seizes him and kisses him, and with impudent face she says to him: "I had to offer sacrifices, and today I have paid my vows: so now I have come out to meet you, to seek you eagerly, and I have found you."

Proverbs 7: 13 – 16

Come and take me in your mouth, lay my head in your lap and
we will make wonders   more, we will make amends
I say this as if it is up to me   is it not you that caresses my face
on days beyond my imagination?   Perhaps in the Judaean desert
or up the road in the Tanami

I am a fallen guy, splintered and left along the fence line
ripped like torn wool on a barbed wire   I live in contradictory
weather   first the heated easterly flush off the desert then
the counter-fugue, a western wind   Indian Ocean medicine

Did you not think I would become addicted to your wine-wise kisses?
Did you not think I would go into your home and take you too?

Like hunger and thirst   perhaps we will hurt each other
but the rain will wash away our iniquity and our concerns

Tomorrow we will be new beings and we will sell our wares
at the market again   perhaps, over the weekend we'll see each other
again and not recognise who we are

Failed Whore

Little black duck, run with me awhile
into yon grassy field   help me to get it
to see how it really is

Crucify me, failed whore, and rebuild me
upon your opium   send me reeling
like a spinning top   read them out loud
your honey words and send them into serious flight
your succorous kisses and settled evening

Blend my futile words with the wide blue sky
hung like a heavy trope on the western edge
teach me the ways of your capricious mind
allow me to wallow in your certain enviable wisdom

Go steady, hardened Zephyr
caress this carcass-heart with care

Asuntos *del corazón*

Break this stick-thing called love · wreck this heart-stone, for what use is it in these times of utter-ness and the weave of the coast just so · Blink and miss it, there on Main Street · instead bless this trivial wink, this insomnia and shuck it back into time, let fold in on itself and pray to Christ it can forgive · Look me in the eye little dog, piss on that parked car's wheel or whatever makes sense because this wintered side of the house no longer does · broad-side this weathered place · Play *Like a Rolling Stone* real slow and quiet but scream it perhaps in a closet along with Beethoven's Adagio cantabile · no more excuses · And you, there across the table, scones, cream and jam between perhaps a stand-in for something lush, perhaps lascivious even and open to the course of the stream we swim in

Waters of the heart

They say the heart is a lost item, a homeless vagabond, retrenched in the aeons, buried at Wounded Knee · Well, some say that · Others, of course, say that this singular muscle is responsible for great cataclysms – wars, plagues, alliances the whole catastrophe in fact and that far from being over, this tiny little vessel will continue its roguish ways indefinitely into the future · trickster, hopeless lover, *Poète Maudit*, lost soul on Philadelphia Avenue

Requite me unrequitable object, there on the altar of Aphrodite or at the feet of Venus or in the tangled hair of Mary Magdalene · Whatever · Miserable prisoner that I am, caught in the web of your conceits, your irresistible urges, penchants, let's say · You have my back little vehicle, you've always had my back, even when you were a smashed cup, a crashed car, an unfixable item on the cracked crazy shelf · Let me repay you with inconsolable grief, a forlorn life, a prism of joy or some such other fascinations along these waters

Va Pensiero

Be my Pavarotti, break my eyes, cut my glass even if this day ends like a falling tree   When children cried and mothers loosed their maternal bonds I tried, I did my best and was found wanting: silent animals came out of the ground to hear that voice and it rained like a lost continent

O Take me back there, before I was, because only without eyes can I really see: only without voice can I even pretend to speak and I have volumes of nothing at all to say and even less to bring to the trench of days, the curvature of decades

If only, if only - yet the reach of each new horizon like those who brought disease, chains, and nothing but genocide on their horses, in their flour sacks   Turn back the clocks   Pavarotti me right in the eyeballs with your *va pensiero*

Let the days roll by, the waves rule, and the sky tear down like some unearthly veil to cover this land: can we remember ever listening to lullabies? Can we see the cattle herded to the slaughterhouse as the blind, in gross innocence follow   follow   follow

Take any organ you can find, hinged in its utter contempt and uselessness, rip them from my throat, those chords and songs, I have no more vectors to guide me – even fate has left the office for the day

If not the sea, the salt air, the sweep of tern or an errant, one-legged gull, then nothing Lord, nothing

The Principle of Limitation (*after Bolleter*)

In this instance, which is neither longer nor shorter
than the smallest distance   is where you will find him
broken piano maestro

The principle allows any instrument, however wrecked or deviated
to be played   to follow its own harmonic
sing its battered sonata   I am a sound strung on
this westerly which flows over the shiny red Vespa parked
here, on smashed Piano Hill

Let me at least screech, chatter, smatter, whisper, whimper
into the bright-dark and disappear   emerge again next year
The Principle of Limitation declares me limited and
unlimited endlessly

Set this Selkie-melody, sleek and melancholy
let it ring under-tone, loud and silent
let this iota-omen beckon
lead the way to secreted, spring-like fresh-water play

Let the music hammer, nay, strain into the demented evening
Am I too not demolished   uttered into slivered pieces
like a lily-livered prophet or small-time god

Busted piano man *(for Ross B)*

His teeth clipped, craggy   pegs of wood, dried bones
the keys have shed their ivory skins peeled like dried gum leaves
amongst which they lay curled   strings, sinew-rusty, over-reached
from under felt fedora his breath hard on the boards

his beloved machines all around   Plaaang, plunk, tink, taaang
zeroing in on the dying moment as they exhale their last
this is their bright shining dark   twanged, plinked
into the unknowing cloud like a monk he squats over them
extracts, extrudes, extrapolates   Exhausted at 3 am. he turns off
the lights, dreams before he sleeps   in his head unrecovered racket
resonant sounds   sonorous, sibilant   silent

busted pianos work overtime deep into the dawn
they have wandered from room to room
he treads the Mobius like a fine-tuned invisible rat
eyes finally glaze as the night claims them   Piano-man
he, they, one   and his seat that squeaks its bit and bees
spiders, mice, ants   chirp, chew, crawl, scree, slink, sluice

honey comb his wiry tendons   play it *sostenuto*

Tomorrow he will become pliant-fingers, ears, cheeks-on-lids

feet-feeling   O the sigh of it   man-piano

see it breathe, this busted thing   hear it groan in the giving of everything

Tomorrow I will receive the CD-gift, run home and play it and play it

missing sounds will invade my eager-child-mind

weeks thereafter made up of three days each instead of seven

the sky mercury water   ground a swell of felt hammers and I

a boy in an empty schoolyard

A day in Marfa (*after Marfa Girl*)

Summer   a rhombille spinning
tumbling round and round like an egg it goes
Sweltering dawn rises   a beautiful butterfly broken

Take stock, write your diary there in Marfa and
here in Mornington   where, it does not matter and
keep the books secure for this day will never again
and yet it will   return
Our crumbling hours like freight trains rumble
tomorrow and each after that

Dusty dry stations have fled like rats in Marfa
into a sinking sand-sea and they come to stand alone
these and those orphaned towns

Sol orbs the earth and sets again
the vesicle wherein we are wombed and graved
We make love, have sex, beget life and again
the dead of day it hums, nay it sings

verily it shouts an elegiacal yawp   shatters dreams and
builds hopes   dashes them as easily as any narcotic can
from which there is no return and although we have found ways
to permanently perpetuate we will still watch as trains thunder by
because, in scorched Marfa, that is where days are forever and we
just as brief and parched this week and next
located like undeniability here and there

We are an eternal circadian rhythm:
just as mayflies gestate for months fly free only a few hours
so too we   only to end on any other given day

Meeting at Tipasa

Could be, here on this peninsula far away from Africa as if from the moon, he and I meet, along the bay: foot prints crossing paths, a glance – we dream of sea creatures: it is the sun on the napes of our necks that unite us in a kind of camaraderie, as if we were brothers who had fought on the same side in the Algerian War and in those trenches we cried and held the other in each other's arms until under the red sun we look up, glance at each other and smile: we are met, here over the black schist and cold grainy shore, by gods of the sea, sun, salt and sand although at Tipasa the gods are more sunburnt and hair more bleached: it's as if Camus was my friend and brother and once we recognised each other the lapping of Port Philip water would remind us both that somewhere, perhaps at Tipasa, we met and tears flowed again in memory of that one, exceptional day.

Port Talbot (*ad honorem Michael Sheen*)

He made a film of the Passion
On a Welsh beach. By day three,
The crucifixion, there were fifteen thousand
At Port Talbot. But what got me,
What really unnerved me
Was the Ecce Homo scene. Jesus
The Welsh actor is asked 'Are you King
Of this town?'   The tension builds
The crowd is live   positively viral,
A full-blown world epidemic.
It is dark: there are cages, police,
Blood-thick air. I don't know
If there was a Jesus thing
Ever   but I know my chest
My skin this day   my threshold
My caesura   the self-breach.
This actor   this man
Full stop on the film of time
Stopped me ?

Left me at the abyss of breath

Retreating to the roaring waves

Of the wild Celtic Sea. They

Lifted him on that beach

Pilate's armies charging by

Dispersing them and they, dropping

Their weapons   becoming farmers

Again: swords, shields into ploughshares.

The stock markets have fallen

Like sinking ships. Maybe it was the same

Way back then. I don't know

If there ever was a Jesus thing

But I know there was this Welsh guy

There, on a dark Leviathan Sea.

Ecce Homo, he cried

I am   he said   here is Man

Strange creature from the Sea

Extracted from dust   Über-Simian

And suddenly I have religion.

Suddenly I am on my knees

Praying to an unbelievable

Yet entirely convincing

Welsh Christ who, like alpha

And omega, tomorrow, will still be here

Whom art has redeemed and who can bridge

This chasm that is my mouth

And suddenly I am that bridge

Broken   collapsed over those stones

On a Port Talbot shore. 'Are you King

Of this town?' Port Talboteans scream

I answer   I am

Art rain

As if Monet himself was sitting there, by my side rain dappling
the windscreen · His *Red Boats at Argenteui*l here overlooking
Tanti Creek mouthing Miller's Beach · A gull, unknowing player,
lands on the car's bonnet · stares me straight in the eye blurred and,
stirred to look seaward, grey rolling waves whitecapped kelpies

Over there, across the sweep of the cove, a neat line of beach houses
colorful as kid's sneakers · the rain bleats still · Monet shudders
like a bird preening itself in the briny estuary waters · this moment
caught in the apparatus of its own making

Mornington

… after dirty rain washed me up and cleansed my train-self · after
it had cleared the clotted blood and the years of not knowing then
the remorse kicked in · I don't know why now · why in the days
of my coastal dwelling where broken schist crumbles like so much
blackened knurl along the Bay's circular path

I guess we cannot choose the fractured moment · the unleashed
news of the day · It is the circling plover's gale-blown gait that
determines our time · we but the jetsam fugue of hours
never to be unravelled

What is this language that limbs its way from arthritis-knuckles
bone-fingers trawling for the right anchorage · This town could not
be dumber in the sound of its jetties, moored boats, gusted sea-salt
and sand · dumb and mute, slowly releasing its secret grip cradled
as it is between Martha and Eliza · slung like a threadbare hammock
curled along a highway that leads to the Southern Ocean

Drops of memory that approach from who knows where but always with unimpeachably impeccable timing · broken as an E harmonica, scaled in descant · helpless things that we are · Mornington, little town along the Bay

Gwen Harwood's Nightfall

From 18 Pine Street, West Hobart she has seen him walking
in the sand   she has seen my grief, joys   my peccadillos
so to speak, and swirled these in her red wine as the southern lights
brit the crepuscule sky   He turns and strolls along
the water unknowingly as she closes the window against Kunanyi's
chilling breeze its jutted ridge attesting this southern nightfall

I kick at sprawled kelp glistening in the rising moonlight
follow the leather of her aged hand   estuary tides and lips
mussels click click with sucking water
plovers screech in dark air above the man who is now lost
in self-reverie   She realises my intensity as we walk together
she, I, them   gulls, sedge, oysters
an ancient fabric, the weight of it all around us shawled

Oyster Cove

Our house is driftwood   graft it, Lord, to the bow of the oncoming
storm and sink into us the words of creation   The natives will steal
into the blinding day, followed by the crack of a claiming pistol into
an echoing distance   Make this a special trial

We did not hear them coming, we did not protect our word
as it leaked across the wintered valley   lend me the primal bush
Putalina and fill the graves with sentiment washed down
in rivers of hurt   Along the shore, beacons on the hilltops

and somewhere, in the break of dunes, the fracture of bone
crust like so many broken middens   so many cracked shells
along coasts of a tomorrow left behind again and then
yesterday and last century they were forgotten

But the places we visit are not, somehow there in the hollow, over
those broken granites, in the blue of the ridge, the wash of the sea
on my battered feet   We should not into the night without our light

the being of Song, heart, our blood even though Wovoka attempts renunciation and mends the broken hoop

Putalina - Oyster Cove, Tasmania

Hobart Town

Kunanyi rests like a rocky, icy shoulder over this place and in its lei the city Van Winkles another hundred years or so, bristles under weighty winds roaring down mountain walls: the town leaves itself open to suggestions that never square off where customers drink boutique beer or special blend coffee, but at each corner secret water from the mountain flows - down diminutive alleyways, around lost bends, under subterranean sluice ways, creeks - smidgen by smidgen what needs to be said is said, but only in another hundred years, perhaps another hundred after that, what needs to be remembered here on this island, under this mountain, perhaps the unsayable, still to be said

Kunanyi - Mt Wellington

Phoenix

Up, along the stretch between Swansea and Bicheno, somewhere around 1981 I reckon, thumbing along the east coast of the Apple Isle: the sun is good to me, the backpack not so bad – the guy says it's been a drought here for seven years and the words don't make sense – drought, seven years, Tasmania. My brain and heart fight desperately for the desert of knowledge and, in several years time I will be married with several kids: the sinews don't get it, the bones are feeling it, and yes, National pies, back in the day, to die for: not so much nowadays where one dies because of. Along that coast dryzabone, further south I lived off the food God-given along the road – apples, blackberries (DDT and all), rosehip, pears you name it , and enough road kill to feed a large family for life. Is it that long between my synapses, my fragile years, eyes and mouth and lips to say these things, to trumpet and herald the news of my self-demise and the phoenix that wings into the skies to allow me one more look?

Wintering with Sei Shōnagon

Sei Shōnagon's *Pillow Book* on the bed
fallen-leaf ochre - *kuchiba* - scattered around our old cottage-home
Snow drift-sky blowing in from the east   cold through
these wooden walls thin as rice paper sliding doors
most excellent winter

She loved the way snow downy layered over the objects of her joy
I love the way she loved and here too the rain falls like gentle sleet

She loved her lists: terrifying things: horrid filthy things:
things that give you confidence: being disliked by others
splendid things: nobles: wells: bridges   Exacting observer
precise as ice-air that brings freshness like a chilly thunderclap
over the peninsula as if a thousand years ago

She smooths her *akome* gown to ensure excellence for her Empress:
in the court of Teishi all was colour, perfect manners, and poetry
Men come and go leaving letters for the courtier women to find

All is flowers: lotus, Kotonashi, wayside grasses, sweet flag, moss

Most honourable behaviour for my lady   Most exquisite image
like a bowl of snow with a sprig of peach blossom-buds
He told her that there is nothing new in any poem
but far more difficult to give the most apt response for each occasion

Golden-rust birch leaves dot our red brick garden path
Dietes: wood iris and lavender most complete
on a most unmitigated winter's day

Lists

… that bring, deliver   break your nerves, your already fragile
resolve   open doors and deliver asteroids to your table like
Lydia Davis's 'could be more comfortable' or Elton John's 'real love
is hard to come by…'   list that!   Love shove shmove
Homonyms, synonyms, antonyms   what is it about
these funny little things   daisy chains of words, ideas, needs
wants, wishes   even planets concentric themselves in your orbit
Mercury, Venus, Earth and beyond them a million moons
a veritable solar system of galaxies

Song me Sei Shōnagon   *your infuriating things   splendid things
horrid filthy things**   lists on a Thursday night and then
for me, first morning things:

muesli and tea for breakfast; read book; chat with daughter # 3; BLT for lunch; PBS Newshour; emails; daughter # 2 and grandkids; work in garden; shopping list; walk the long way to the shop to keep up steps; make dinner; noodles, bacon, sauce; Rick Stein's Cornwall; Elton John –

it's sad, so sad

Sei Shōnagon asleep on my lap
Rocket man on my mind

* From Sei Shōnagon's Pillow Book

Kundera

At the end of Kundera's unimaginable book The Unbearable
Lightness of Being I come across five empty pages (in the faber
and faber edition)   I imagine all sorts of other endings he could
have written, like Tereze and Tomas make it and live happily forever
spoiler alert   they don't
The thing about imagination is how real it is   how visceral
like the way the pain my knee feels after that gravel rash bites in

It's funny how French Island is still there even if I never saw it like
Tereze and Tomas really didn't die in that horrendous car crash
O how I could fill those final last five pages...

Perhaps I will make some notes as to how the story ends
the second time I have read this book and still feel all those imaginary
things I had previously felt about all the unimaginable happenings
that somehow accidentally poured forth from the very real mind of
a Czech writer   like the way another faraway island
called Rottnest I imagine only because I've been there a hundred times

De l'amour

Undone eggs over fresh-morning tomatoes and
first of the seven fulfilments of Stendhal's l'amour is met
… admiration

Add salt and pepper, oregano and thyme straight out of the garden
how delightful to be kissed by the dawn and
the second fulfilment met   there are five more

Parmigiano parsley and you can forget the rest of his ingredients

Steal the whole recipe from his book De l'amour where, in droves
he speaks of glances, barbarians, Provence, thunderbolts
where he writes her name, Metilde, in the margins   all the margins
Metilde who gives him the cold shoulder in favor of another
when her young life of thirty-five completed seasons ends

Have I told you lately that I love you   bite me I beg you, eat me
eat me and my breakfast with you and when you are done

throw the plate to break on the kitchen wall

so no one else may feast from it   reject me one more time so that

I can scribe it in this recipe, let the parsley tell me some more

let the spices and juices follow me all my ending days.

Accept

She lets her head on his shoulder, her eyes in the sky over them both bough of tree scraping at the tin roof and the round-grey watery clouds clustered as the room fills with winter's-dark: into the kitchen window

escaped sun as she watches smoke bilge from a chimney down the road and for the first time he understands, as he lets his heart, her hand warm as a caress, accept and he drinks the care of it in

Little gargoyle (*for Esther*)

Out of child's mind born: guardian plaything. Goggle-eyed, devil-horned facing northern winter-sun   sharp winged shadows on winter's deck   protect us. One day this headache will end, this halo-torc - golden broken. Too long ago, our children played, way back then, little gargoyle, what do you say to that?

Pay the Time-Lord, relate me back to my blistered hands, the dirt beneath my nails: raise that roof, shift that clay: arrange   arrange me with your masterfully made sharp tiny teeth, pound me with your substantial paws little gargoyle   feed me your home-garden vegetables be watchful over my seedlings, see if we don't all make it in the long race, the sharp distance into the sunset.

Stay your star-fixed eyes, bulging, or are you smiling secretly as your maker intended   do you comprehend things I cannot begin to know? Stake my tomatoes, wipe my sweat-brow, guardian. Child's plaything. Lonely little goddess.

Child's heart

Did lead fall from the sky like molten drops of rain, cut through the week of our days and cross roads when we were kids raising kids: decades of our mornings festoon the scroll of memories long-forgotten recall at slip of secret code word opened and the door to then when kith and kin around the hearth, candles and cake   birth, death, gathering: dragon-breath mornings rugged up or summer evening basketball and tears, triumph or loss: didn't lead drop when a child's heart scattered like so much regolith and like so much sand through a sensory sieve, water-bridge   no bird coop but the sun like a lance breaks through blanket-cloud eventually and those days   cake and icing.

Marj and Harvey (*in memoriam*)

Broken, scattered twigs in just the right place:
no electricity, and shitloads of mozzies
the earth on their property is moved but only by hand and twilight
is their home   the place used to be a slaughterhouse and now:
Ashram's meditators, gurus, and acolytes

Ephebe, listen when I tell you about long summer afternoon-walks
home and tales from long ago, Hatha Yoga and secret signs: oneiric
symbols and when poetry began: 'twas a gay science that thing with
words that grew from black boys, red gums, ghost gums, postman's
runners, Mulla Mullas, and all matters gravel and bauxite in the hills
east of the city, there on the far horizon, a strudel scrolling along
the scarp deep into the south

Listen to Marj, spritely sprite, who taught patience, love: the care
for all things in their rightful place, the earth and Harvey, penitent
who missed his fragile wren, after she had gone into the night:
after many hours in the dark: the house rickety still-standing

becomes them and the silence and the bush and granite and ants and flies   they-I are one and the earth subsumes us on Margaret Road

Meditation upon Hexagram 32 Heng

Chen above   arousing thunder
Sun below   gentle wind
Duration   *Success*   *Perseverance*

                                                    I Ching

Sunset diastole in the shimmer-light of evening
leaf-fall · who let the soldiers in?   please refrain from
prophecy and breaststroke · understand the rounds of seconds
and the hemi-sphere of dawn-music

the persistence of grey-window days · remove the doubt of night
refer to my childhood, blue trumpets and xylophones
the arc of mandolin and, above all, endure
gentle winter-smoke over trees ripple · shine like thick rope

Please inform Marg Smith, I will see her soon
and our mate, Harvey, there at the bend on Margaret Road
where I once lived · turn and down the hill

Whenever the dust of the road raises questions

leave it all · doubt · self-fingers · toes

leave them · run like the stallion

pay homage to the ancestors and call in the firefighters

who let the soldiers in · the army has returned home

Duration   *Success*   *Perseverance*

Crazy man

A grandchild anticipates a mother's belly, she is pregnant with waiting, that baby, the mother a child still ... do we ever grow ... up: planes take their flight around us, their passengers trust, disembark, arrive in the ports of the world nestled in some distant-star corner: we played and played like crazy people, ruff and tumble ... sprawled, getting the measure of each, testing the ground to see it won't collapse beneath us

we hold, are held and sometimes dropped – the earth too is a cushion made of umber and scratch and bleed, it scorches, nurtures, gestates, grows us, firms us up for future gens and my child's child's child will eat dirt too, just to check it out to see it tastes as good as it did to our ancestors far away in some middle Europa when Roman's ruled and before them the Celts wandered: crazy man, wander and walk this earth some more, come home when you are ready.

Sun, Sun

As in, shine on, shine on you baublely thing, to the ocean's edge, sinking into a vast sea along this coast · as in, happy O day and the children and the dog the smell of frying stuff or oils and salads, bodies the whole semiotic thang · As in, I shoulda · told you more often · I shoulda said, let you know, should not have underestimated you, not read you wrong, trusted more perhaps

Let the gods have their way, instead of trying to control the whole damn thing · as in ? I'm such an idiot · if only, if · only if, and we can't go back can we · I'm not conjecturing here, I'm pleading, letting go, laying myself on the line · My head on the block, heart on my tattoo-sleeve

Shine on, shine on, happy O day, on this vast Indian Ocean edge to Africa · The next thing you 'll see will be the sluicing triangles on the backs of watery beasts, circling, circling · circling · The next time round, no more 'I coulda's' or 'I shoulda's' · only I will · power is not a bad thing, if we've got it, right · only how you use it

Delight

... make the world go away ... *   she sings

it is there in that vacant lot I can anchor myself

find enough room to breathe lightly

anger dissipates   carefree smiles, move in

Is it not good to feel so

to sleep with ease   to digest this world-stuff

... going to the chapel and we're goning to get married...*

they chant   it is my day to be happy

The dark gods have left and who are we to refuse the cup

to reject the gift of Grace   the spritely step

* *Make the world away* as sung by Elvis

* *Going to the chape*l as sung by The Dixie Cups

Acknowledgements

I would like to thank the editors of the following journals or online sites and other publications that have supported me by accepting many of these poems for publication:

Tamba, 2017: Cuttlefish, 2018: Locus: OOTA Anthology 2019: Poetry d'amour, 2019, 2020, 2023: Westerly, 2019: Mozzie 2021, 2022: Brushstrokes II Anthology 2021: writ.Poetry Review 4, 2020: The Honest Ulsterman, 2021: Blind summits, 2021: Azuria, 2022: Mozzie, 2021, 2022, 2023 : Brushstrokes III, 2022: Cordite 108, 2023: Cuttlefish 2023; Westerly 68.1, 2023

Awards

Several of these poems have won awards including:

Port Talbot *Second Prize Patrons Prize 2014*
The Menagerie *Highly Commended Patrons Prize 2017*
Va Pensiero *Shortlisted Tom Collins 2017*
Busted Piano *Man First Prize Tom Collins 2018*

www.ingramcontent.com/pod-product-compliance
Lightning Source LLC
Chambersburg PA
CBHW020537080526
44583CB00013B/895